Talking with the Women

Travels Across Rwanda, Congo, Burundi, and Uganda

Nov-Dec. 2014

Cindy Garris

This is a work of history. Historical individuals and places and events are mentioned.

Copyright © 2022 by Cynthia Garris

Published by Revivalfire Ministries

ISBN 13:978-1-7377944-7-9

*All rights reserved.
No part of this book may be used or reproduced in any manner whatsoever, without written permission, except in the case of brief quotations embodied in critical articles and reviews, as provided by US Copyright Law.*

*For information, address
<u>dale@revivalfire.org</u>*

First paperback printing February 2022

Printed in the United States of America

Table of Contents

Talking With the Women

Day 1-5: Kigali and Rwanda. 1

Day 6:   Kigali to Bukavu, Burundi.   4

Days 7-10: Three Day Conference   8

Day 11 & 12: Chai Church, Bukavu   10

Day 13 & 14:   Bukavu. Yvette   12

Day 18: Sandra at Gitegi and Burundi   14

Day 19: Sunday night.   18

Day 20-Day 23: , Rwanda   19

Day 24:   Travels with Emmanuel   20

Day 28: Mbarara, Uganda   24

Day 29: Esther Kamanzi's testimony   26

Day 29:   Banana Plantation Church   28

Day 31: Uganda with Peter   30

Day 32: Elivaat Butare 2nd Day   33

Day 35 & 36: Kigondo   36

Day 37: Ladies of Hope Meeting   40

Day 38: Wedding Customs   43

Day 38, 39, and 40: Kampala   46

Day 1-5: Charlotte in Kigali, Rwanda with Isaiah.

Forty women attended this meeting. Charlotte is a pastor's wife who moved to Rwanda from Kenya in March 2014. The Lord dealt with them to move to Rwanda permanently and minister with a specific church here. They sold everything and left their 9- & 10-year-old girls with Charlotte's mom to finish out the school term in Kenya. She was six months pregnant when she arrived, and she didn't speak the Rwanda language. Friends in Kenya thought she and her husband were crazy for moving, but she told them God's plans do not always make sense to us.

I was impressed by her testimony for many reasons. Here is a native African Christian moving to a different African country to minister to other African women. I think Americans tend to think of Africa as a whole unit when actually there are many countries with many cultures, tribes, and languages per country. Charlotte wanted to encourage the women in this meeting to listen to the Lord. When He deals with you to do something different, He always gives you what you need to prosper. Prosper can mean spiritual, financial, and many other things. He will bless your endeavors even if it is a struggle or hard work to make a move like this successful. She made friends, found help and gave help, and backed up her husband while he ministered in this new country. And God gave her a translator while she was in labor and delivery. Yes--they do have their babies in hospitals and clinics! (I asked!)

Charlotte also felt like the Lord hears women's prayers faster because their hearts are softer! She said she felt that way, especially when she was pregnant. You never know what kind of servant of God you are carrying close to your heart. They did say that, in general, they think American women don't have problems. I asked them why on earth they would think that! Everybody has problems. And if you are saved, Satan will attack you because

Talking With the Women

he wants you to go to hell.

The women are always excited and thrilled by the end of their meeting when Dale shows up for the evening revival service. He asked if I knew why the women's meetings go so well. I am not sure, especially since they don't always talk or open up like Charlotte. I think when we all realize that whether we are Rwandan, Kenyan, or American, our hearts want the same things: love, security, etc. We find a common bond regardless of our circumstances. When we are born again of the Spirit, the bond with the Lord connects us even more. How we read His Word, how He helps us overcome, and how we seek Godly counsel make all the difference in the world. I can't imagine what kind of life I would have without Jesus. So maybe that is why these meetings seem so good to these women? I don't know, but I always hope (wonder) if I make a difference and a lasting effect.

Cindy Garris

Day 6:
The ride from Kigali to Bukavu, Burundi.

It's usually little kids in the backseat asking this question. But it was me in the backseat asking this last night. How much farther? Are we there yet?

Our ride from Kigali, Rwanda to Bukavu, Congo, should have only taken 3 ½ to 4 hours. But

Talking With the Women

with one mistake at the beginning of the trip and a series of other unfortunate events (or comedy of errors-whichever you prefer), our ride took 12 hours. And we didn't even make it to Bukavu. Our host (Isaiah) has a taxi driver that he uses, and he arranged our ride. But he misunderstood where we were going and told his driver to go to the border of Goma, Congo, instead of the border at Bukavu.

Two hours into the ride, Dale noticed some traffic signs and realized we were going north instead of south. We told the driver (even before we left the hotel) we were going to Bukavu, but all he understood was to take the Americans to the border at Goma. Ahhh, here we are in Goma. Our interpreter and contact people at the church are calling us from Bukavu wondering where we are. They are ready to pick us up. You are in Goma? What are you doing there?

The driver (who speaks very little English) didn't want to drive us to Bukavu, but he did. How long to get there from Goma? About four hours. OK, not a problem. We will pay you more money to take us there. So begins the adventure! Wrong city, language barrier, road conditions, serious speed bumps, "S" curves up and down the mountain, no network connection to communicate, phone time running out, battery running low, no bathroom facilities (for me), and more. Four hours later—how much farther? ANOTHER three hours, really?! The border closes at 6 PM, so what do we do now?

At 6 PM, it's already dark. I don't handle the night darkness well, especially traveling forever on miles and miles of "S" curves, through the National Gorilla Forest, with some good roads but lots of construction and gravel roads halfway through the forest. I thought, is this ever going to end? I made sure not to drink anything before we left at 10 AM, but now it is 7 PM. NO civilization; NO lights except oncoming cars and trucks. NO anything! I hung in until about 9 PM, and then little tears started running down my face. Dale knew, but he didn't want to press the issue.

I started praying for light in the darkness. I started praying for our driver. Dale asked if he was tired; Bosco said, "No! I am strong!" (I thought, OK for you.) I started praying very specific requests — a place for me, a hotel, any village or town with lights, get off this road, find a traffic sign with information, good phone connection, someone who speaks English!

At last, the communication picked up between our interpreter (Etienne) and our driver (Bosco). Etienne called us about every hour checking our progress. Evidence of life started showing up after we finally got out of the forest. People in Bukavu were looking for a hotel for us so we could spend

Talking With the Women

the night somewhere close and then finish the trip. Etienne found someone to meet us in Cyangugu at 10 PM, make arrangements at the hotel, and pick us up in the morning. We paid Bosco for his room and the extra driving time and headed for a hot shower and our room.

The next morning, we had a thankful prayer hour! When Dale looked up our route, we discovered Bosco missed the turn for the direct road from Goma to Bukavu, and that took us the long way through the gorilla forest. Ahh—just part of the adventure.

Here are the scriptures that helped: Psalm 112:4; Psalm 119:105; Isaiah 42:16; and John 8:12. Even though I could see no light at the end of the road, He brought His Word to me in the darkness, and now I have a story to tell!

Cindy Garris

Days 7-10:
Three Day Conference in Bukavu, Congo

There was time for questions and answers that really turned up the intensity of the meetings. Lots of questions were good ones, but there were a couple directed at me. You have heard me talk about the dress code—this was in full force for these men. I had a hard time with some of this stuff because there are scriptures to back up a couple of things these men asked. This time it was women

Talking With the Women

wearing makeup. (At a meeting in the spring with this same denomination, the question involved the head covering, the trousers, and the submission to men thing.) The second day when another pastor asked Dale about women wearing makeup, Dale said (I love him for this!): Good God Almighty! What is wrong with you men? People are living and dying in sin, and going to hell out there on the street and you are worried about a woman in the church wearing makeup?

Cindy Garris

Day 11 & 12:
Mirielle - Chai Church, Bukavu, Congo

Mireille was my translator for this woman's meeting; I met her last spring at the young married women's meeting in Penuel Church. The women at this church meet Monday from 7 AM to 9 AM for prayer and again on Wednesday from 7 AM to 9 AM for Bible reading. Unfortunately for all of us, some breakdown of communication happened, and I showed up at 9 AM on Wednesday, and they didn't even know I was coming!

They were almost finished, and a few of them were preparing to travel to Goma (yep! That famous ride) for a women's conference, so we didn't have a lot of time together. We had thirty

Talking With the Women

minutes to talk. We hit the high points: giving my testimony, reading and praying together, which they obviously did, having a solid group of women for support and encouragement. Not much, but Mireille has emailed me every week since we left!

Day 13 & 14: Bukavu, Congo. Yvette

I talked to Yvette on the last day of this Congo conference. I also met her in the spring at Penuel Church. She has been married for two years, and they do not have a baby yet. She does not have a job either. I remember Diana (Noah's wife) telling me pressure is applied after you have been married a while and do not get pregnant. The same was happening to Yvette. Two years is a very long time to not have a baby.

I don't know which family members and friends had started pressuring Yvette, but she was obviously distraught. We prayed. I didn't really

Talking With the Women

have any answers for her. God is the giver of life; who are we to say when He should give it? But that didn't make Yvette feel better. Michel, our host, says that is another attitude they are praying to change. A woman is considered cursed or worse if she doesn't produce a child in pretty short order.

Women have few job opportunities and choices. If they have the opportunity for an education, they can be schoolteachers, secretaries, office workers, typists, etc. Restaurants and hotels hire women who have attended colleges of hospitality. Mireille took five years of language at the University in Bukavu, and she speaks four languages fluently. She is employed by Humanitarian Services (not sure what all that means!). She took off work that morning to translate for me.

Our taxi driver waited for us since our meeting was so short. Mireille rode back to the church with me so I could join Dale. Then—in her fancy African dress—she hopped on a motorbike and went to work! I am wondering in Yvette's particular situation as a young pastor's wife, what can she do to earn money? Are there restrictions for her? This CEPAC group is so stringent; there are probably things she cannot do. I wonder what the women in Burundi face? I will find out soon enough.

Cindy Garris

Day 18:
Sandra at Gitegi and Burundi

Sandra was my translator here. Pastor Lambert pressed her into translating as "her service to the Lord." When I found out she was my interpreter, I was a little concerned. Her English was OK, but I really wanted someone who was more fluid than her. I am glad that I didn't push to get someone else because God had it all worked out. There was another woman in the group who would help her out when she got stuck. Now she feels confident that she faced this challenge and conquered her fears. She is ready to try it again with someone else.

At the women's meeting, we talked about the usual things—reading and praying with each other in small groups, older women mentoring younger women, and praying for unsaved souls. They felt that American women have no problems, and life is always rich and good. True, we have no wars on our land, no extreme poverty, and more freedom for women, but we still have needs that are important and need prayer.

Approximately 80 women were there. I have found that if I make eye contact with each one and acknowledge them individually in some way that they feel special. They think I am coming to preach, but they find out I am a regular person just like

Talking With the Women

them. It seems each meeting ends up about the same—we are friends.

Sandra's husband, Anthony, is Italian! He has lived all over the world, moved to Burundi ten years ago, and is a peacekeeper for the UN. They have been married for about seven years. He has children by a previous marriage—some are grown, but he has Samuel, who is 11, and they have Suzanna, who is five. Remember the "Jungle Book" movie? Suzanna wrinkles her nose just like Mowgli did! Suzanna is not afraid to try or do anything and is not afraid to ask any questions. She noticed the hair on Dale's arms (my daddy has hair like that!) and asked about my freckles. Anthony and Sandra had us to their house for dinner twice and drove us to the airport Sunday evening.

When Sandra goes to the local market, they

know she is the wife of a white man, so they wonder if she will talk to them. But she witnesses to them, tells them her testimony, and brings them to church to get saved. The Lord showed her one time that she would work with a white woman in the future and help the women in her country! The Lord also used her to pray for two women, one who had cancer, and they got healed!

One more fun thing: we went fabric shopping the day after the first service. The woman that I bought the fabric from was at the service! I couldn't find her the next day when I went to buy more fabric. Everyone wanted to charge me twice as much as she did. She was at the women's meeting, and I was so happy to see her there! We joked and

Talking With the Women

laughed, and I asked her to bring me another six yards, and I would pay her. Any color, any print—just more fabric, please! I had my money and a thank you note ready for her after Sunday services. She brought me six more yards as a gift—no charge!

Cindy Garris

Day 19: Sunday night.

It was time to drive back to Bujumbura from Gitegi and fly to Kigali, Rwanda to spend a week with Emmanuel, Noah's brother.

Anthony, Sandra, and Suzanna drove us the 3-hour ride to the airport. Another couple from the Gitegi church met us at the airport to say goodbye. AMAZING! What a huge blessing this church and its people were for us. It was on this ride that I started making notes of all the different signs, slogans, and observations to write the "trivia" emails.

Day 20-Day 23: Kiramurzi and Kabarondo, Rwanda

We visited two village churches that were a 2-hour drive one way from Kigali. There was no time to have any woman's meeting at either place. Dale had to condense the messages for these churches because only two services were scheduled. He usually asks me to say a few words; I keep it pretty short. The bishop of Kabarondo asked me to come back Sunday to have my own women's meeting! I looked at Dale and Emma and said: I can't. We are already scheduled for another church in Kigali. He asked again—I honestly didn't know what to say! Sorry, but no.

On the ride back to Kigali, Dale was laughing so hard. He told Emma there was no way I would travel two hours away when he would be at another church. And who was going to translate since Emma was doing it for both of us! Poor Emma—he really wanted to please everybody and just didn't understand why I wouldn't do it.

Cindy Garris

Day 24:
Travels with Emmanuel and Rwanda Trivia

Rwanda is incredibly beautiful: *The Land of a Thousand Hills* with tea fields and sugar cane as far as you can see. There are miles and miles of highway in the mountains with tea fields and walking paths. People are scattered everywhere digging, bagging, and sorting tea. They all have a special basket on their back, and some have a hoe or shovel over their shoulders. Where do they come from? How do they get there?

One pretty cool thing that I haven't seen anywhere else: very tall trees with what looks like a woven bamboo mat (actually papyrus) all rolled up and tied way up in the tree. Emma said these are beehives! I don't know who puts them up there and how they harvest the honey, but they are spaced about three trees apart on the edges of the tea fields.

Bicycles and motorbikes are everywhere: in the city and villages and in every country. They carry people and transport goods. *One bicycle can carry:* ten Jeri cans (yellow 5-gallon plastic jugs), water or cooking oil, 40 + pineapples, two mattresses rolled up and tied on the back tire, a huge stack of wood or a wooden door, along with two or more people! On several roads, guys would be riding a bicycle and hanging onto the fender of a truck riding up the steep mountain road getting a "free" ride. They would also do the same coming down—and that is scary because these are steep, curvy roads. *One motorcycle can carry:* a wooden bed frame, three to five people plus the driver, crates of produce, three

Cindy Garris

sacks of charcoal, on and on.

PAY ME MY MONEY: We stopped at a market to get some water and use the public restrooms. The next day we stopped again at the same place, and a girl ran up to Dale demanding him to give her "her" money!

Dale: What are you talking about? (He's thinking to himself: you want all my money? You are brave or foolish; I am twice as big as you.)

Girl: You owe me money! You owe me 100 shillings.

Dale: For What?

Girl: You must pay to use the toilet. Give me my money!

Emma: Dale, didn't you know you must pay? Didn't you pay yesterday?

Dale: No, I didn't know. Here is your money! (We all had a good laugh in the car on the way to the church. 100 Rwanda shillings are about 15 cents.)

SUNBURN: Emma: I hear white people get red skin if they are out in the sun too long. Is that true!

Me: Yes—it's called sunburn.

Emma: I have seen white people get red in the face when they are angry or upset too!

Me: Yes—that's also true (maybe he was thinking about when Dale got mad at him about a couple of things?!).

Talking With the Women

Me: Did you know that if your sunburn is really bad, that your skin peels off a few days later?

Emma: WHAT! Your skin comes off? That is really weird!

LOVEBIRD: Most of the time on these long drives, Dale takes a nap. Emma and Pastor Miriam are chattering away practically non-stop. When Dale and I did talk, we would start poking and laughing at each other. When we saw the guy walking down the street with a bright yellow t-shirt that said in big black letters: "MY FEET HURT!"; we couldn't stop laughing. Everyone walks everywhere!

Emma: What are you two lovebirds laughing about now?

Dale: What does that mean: lovebirds? We aren't doing anything.

Emma: You are always laughing and having fun with each other.

Dale: Should we pray for you to find a wife, Emma?

Emma: WHAT? NO. No. What are you saying to me anyway?

Day 28:
Lakeview Resort Hotel, Mbarara, Uganda

I am looking outside my hotel window at the big lawn, papyrus, trees, and lake at the hotel. I woke up to hear one of the gardeners running the weed-eater. That's how they "mow" the lawn at this hotel. I also see two women sweeping the grass cuttings into little piles to bag it up and use it for mulch somewhere. At least they are using the straw brooms that have long handles and not the short handles where they always bend over from their waist to sweep parking lots. It drives me crazy!

The lake has papyrus in it. It is tall with a big puff at the top. It makes me think of a giant green dandelion going to seed! It also reminds me of Dr.

Talking With the Women

Seuss's books! Basket-weaver birds have a colony in a tree beside the lake. They are bright yellow, green, and blackbirds that weave their nests so they look like an upside-down basket! They flutter their wings and dance for the females to come to their nest. They steal grass and weavings from the other male's nests when they want the same female bird! These birds are noisy and constantly flying to the papyrus to bring long skinny grass to weave and knot around a tree twig to build their nest. Amazing to watch! No evolution in this design!

Day 29:
Esther Kamanzi's testimony

I met Esther on a previous trip. While we were at Lakeview Resort, I heard more of her testimony.

Esther is an orphan from Rwanda. When her parents were killed in the genocide, she was "adopted" by a man and his wife who raised her and gave her an education. She was protected by God and fortunate to have someone raise her as their own child. She has done many different things to educate herself; one is attending the College of Hospitality. She traveled back to Rwanda to see if any of her family was still alive and contacted a sister and an uncle. The uncle tried to trick her, and she was almost sold into a false marriage so her uncle could gain the cows from her dowry. Something got delayed, and while she was waiting in a house for her uncle to return, a neighbor warned her and told her to run and hide. She spent the night hiding in bushes and worked her way back to Uganda to get away.

She met Jennifer, a Christian woman from the UK, who mentored her and prayed with her about her past tragedies. When Esther met David in Uganda, they became friends. Three years later, he asked her to marry him, but she was afraid and bitter. Jennifer helped her through that, and she and David had a simple ceremony. Her uncle died a short time after her wedding to David, but she refused to go to the burial because she hated him so much.

David and Esther have been married for five years. Now they have three boys of their own, several orphans, and a happy marriage! David already was caring for seven orphan boys when she met him. I think I would have been hesitant also!

When Dale came to Rwanda and Uganda a few years ago, he preached the revival message. But he found there needed to be healing and forgiveness in people's hearts concerning the Rwandan genocide. Esther and David had been married about one year, and through this message, Esther's heart began to heal.

She and David teach all the young people in their care how to be a family, make a living, and the Bible. David also pastors a church in a different area of Mbarara, and Esther teaches different classes and sells jewelry to help support themselves.

Day 29:
Picture Day and Banana Plantation Church

This morning is specifically to take pictures of the Home of Hope children. We talked about what to call them—not orphans anymore. Finally decided that they are a family, so it is the HOH family or kids!

Now, driving time again! I thought the afternoon church service was in Mbarara, but it was "not too far away." I don't even know the name of the place, but once we got off the main highway, we drove on a good dirt road, then a rough dirt road, then a bumpy dirt path. Dale asked Noah: where ARE we going? We are inside a banana plantation!

Talking With the Women

Dale took pictures—banana trees as far as you could see. Little houses, people with banana bunches on their bikes, a few cows, and lots of goats tethered to trees. Noah turned the car around a couple of times, and we asked him if he knew where he was going! Some little kids saw us and yelled at Noah: "Pastor, Pastor. Church is this way! Follow us!" They ran in front of the car because we were going so slowly on this bumpy goat path. They took us to a mud building (hard as a rock) with no doors or windows—just open spaces. I am not sure how many fit in that small building, but it was packed. A bamboo mat was on the floor with some wooden benches and some old upholstered chairs for the pastors in the front! The Spirit flowed all around. One animal hide drum, a few singers and dancers, and a happy congregation ready for a revival message! What a day.

Day 31:
Bushenyi-Butare, Uganda with Peter

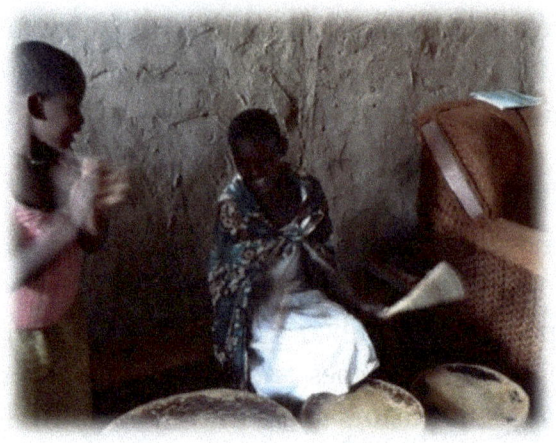

It is so funny when the men realize they are not invited to the women's meetings! They simply are not used to that. Even Dale has only been to one meeting. Sometimes there is no woman who speaks English, so Noah or one of his brothers has been there to translate for me. Peter had all the men go outside to a covered area near the church. Poor Dale—he was not prepared to talk, but he did. I think they basically just had a question and answer session. We just never know what is going to happen.

I have a basic format, and then I wait to see what direction our conversations take from there. I give

Talking With the Women

my testimony, talk about the importance of reading the Bible with each other and holding each other up in prayer. I tell them how strong they are and how much I respect them. Then I wait to see if anyone will give me their testimony.

They were quiet, so I went through the group and just did random picks—they loved that! I handed them the microphone and said: 'What is your name?" I would shake their hand, repeat it, and then make them say my name. "How long have you been saved?" "What do you want to do for God?" Giving them three basic questions controlled the length of time they talked and gave more women a chance to be acknowledged and recognized. I tease, joke around, and just make friends with them. Some of the stuff they tell me truly takes me by surprise.

Cindy Garris

I had two women translating: Pastor Eliva and Deborah—the youngest Kamanzi daughter. It was like a family reunion at Peter's church! Deborah is 21. I handed the front row two notebooks, and they wrote their names and their children's names down. I told them I would bring their names back, and we would pray for them. (This also gave me a count of how many women were there. I wish I had thought of this at the other places.)

I asked them questions about courtship, dowries, and wedding customs. I found out some interesting stuff...not just from them but asking Noah questions on the way to the airport a few days later. I was a little off-balance to begin with, but I had another meeting with the same women the next day. I wasn't sure how I was going to fill up another hour the next day. I shouldn't have worried! It all worked out.

Day 32:
Elivaat Butare 2nd Day

Most African women, no matter what country, are treated as second-class people. The Lord showed me they needed to see that they were important to Him just because of who they were. I read a book called 12 Extraordinary Women, and Mary Magdalen is the one who I have used several times when speaking to these women.

Even though she is mentioned only a few times in the gospels, Jesus acknowledged her publically because she truly worshipped Him. She had seven demons cast out of her! She ministered to Him as He traveled through the countryside. She stayed at the cross and watched where His body was taken to be buried. She prepared spices and returned to anoint Him properly. How did He honor her during her lifetime, and how did He honor her in the Bible? She was the first person He talked to after He rose from the dead! These women never realized Jesus spoke to Mary Magdalene first--even before His apostles.

Cindy Garris

On the 2nd day with this group of women, I asked who had read their Bible that day. Out of 200 women, only a few raised their hands. Mary Magdalen was their example again. Why did Mary follow Jesus everywhere? So she could hear His words and teachings. She felt the power and authority and the life in His words. Mary had to remember everything He said. God has given us His Word, the Bible, so we can read it and study it anytime we want to. Who knows if she could even read? Do we not feel the need to have Jesus' words in front of us every day? Don't we think it is important to read every day so we can have Jesus talk to us?

They promised they would read more from now on! This was the service where people came to the

Talking With the Women

altar and prayed like I have never seen or felt before. I can't even describe it. Heart-rending? Dale, Noah, Peter, and I went through the crowd and just prayed and touched everyone.

Pastor Eliva—my translator—was on her face before the pulpit praying and crying so hard, I just sat down next to her and prayed along with her. I squeezed in and out of the people and touched different women and prayed holding their hands. A couple of women who were so stoic and deadpan during our meetings pulled my hands over to them so I could touch them and pray at the altar with them. That surprised me because I just never know what some of them are thinking.

Cindy Garris

Day 35 & 36:
Katie and Miriam at Kigondo

We are back at the Cielo Country Inn in Ishaka-Bushenyi. The next two days will be at a "church plant" of Peter's. This is another church in the middle of a banana plantation! What is interesting is: this was not the original church we were scheduled for. A bridge that we had to cross collapsed on Sunday and was not able to be repaired by Tuesday. I don't know what kind of bridge or why it collapsed. Maybe because it is the rainy season and things get muddy and soggy? Whatever the reason, I am glad it happened before we crossed it and not during or after it collapsed!

Now I know what the mud-brick homes look like inside. The front room is about 8 ft. x 8 ft. They have a small coffee table with six blue plastic chairs surrounding it. A calendar was nailed to the wall. There was a wooden door with a very large sliding lock on it. A set of wooden shelves was home to their eating utensils and food supply. This had a fabric curtain covering it. An open doorway with another fabric curtain separated this front room from the rest of the house. They cook outside over an open fire with a pot and pan. Katie served us something different at each meal: some boiled chicken or goat meat in a red broth, rice, potatoes,

Talking With the Women

and the cooked banana dish. Fruit: pineapple, oranges, and fresh bananas. They put a plastic tub on the floor, give you a bar of soap, and pour warm water from a pitcher over your hands so you can wash before and after your meal. This is Katie's (the Pastor's wife) home.

There were 72 women at this meeting; 50 directly from that church, and the others from Peter's main church in town or others who just walked from the houses around the area. Some came from six miles away. Pretty good attendance considering this was not the original church we were scheduled for!

These women were not shy at all! I gave my testimony, passed the notebook around for them to write their names, and then called on several of them to give their testimony. Miriam was my translator. She was from Peter's main church; 21 years old and had never done this before. She was nervous but she picked up the flow right away.

I told them how strong they were—walking, carrying things on their heads with their babies on their backs! I tried to walk with my Bible on my head but it slipped off. They all laughed.

I would pick someone from the crowd and hand her the microphone. One woman had been saved 4 years—the Lord healed her from being crazy—(her words). Another woman had been saved for seven years; she was deaf and couldn't see very well. The

Cindy Garris

Lord healed her when she got saved. Three others got up and told me their name, how long they have been saved, and what they wanted to do for God. When I asked for prayer requests, most of them named a husband or family member to either get saved or be deeper in the Lord.

They all agreed that they felt on a personal level that they, and women in general, were special to God. Women could be important to themselves and God as a person. They work hard but don't appear as downtrodden as the women in the Congo. We talked about how they needed to pray for the Congo women. They said they knew American women have problems and even if they are not the same as their issues, that we all needed prayer and answers from God. Then they asked how they could pray for me!

Only five women had Bibles. I told them the ones who had Bibles had a responsibility to read with

Talking With the Women

the ones who didn't. Even Proverbs and Psalms would bind them together as a unit and make them stronger. Pass the Bible around the group and give everyone a chance to hold the Word in their hands and see it with their eyes. God will honor their effort and give them grace, power, and strength. Maybe by seeing their efforts, He will work it out to get them more Bibles! Bibles cost $8.00 which is about 21,000 shillings. For some of them, that is one week's pay. We purchased 18 Bibles for this second banana plantation church as well as the church that Noah took us to. Pastor Emmanuel assured us he would prayerfully distribute these. Sometimes when a Bible or anything free is given away, there are hurt feelings if there is not enough to go around.

At the final church service, Pastor Emmanuel put his arm around his wife Katie and told the congregation how he appreciated her and how God had blessed him. That was really special. Men generally don't publicly praise their wives, and all the women clapped for them! When Peter asked for the church tithe, he also said for them to pray and whatever they were able to give, bring to the servants of God. Many people came up to Dale and me and pressed coins into our hands. When we got back to the hotel, the total was about $5.00. My translator gave me a 2000 shilling note. That is about 75 cents.

Cindy Garris

Day 37: Ladies of Hope Meeting

It has taken almost two weeks of being in Mbarara before I finally got to see some of the Ladies. Noah said now they call themselves the Women of Peace!

Twenty-two women were able to come. I knew there would not be a lot because they have either moved to a different area or have a job! I saw some of them at two different markets—several at the sewing booth and a few more at the hairdressing salon. I am pretty excited about both places. They are sharing the rental cost and space with another business that sews school uniforms. They have very tight quarters, but they are doing well. Fabric is hanging on the walls, zippers and threads are on display, and all the machines were humming! They are now sewing custom clothes and dresses too.

Talking With the Women

The hair salon was in a row with three others, but all of them had customers. It takes six months to learn the different ways to weave their hair; some of them take another six months of training and will be able to do anything when they are done. The LOH had two customers who were having their hair done while they were sitting on the floor as I talked to them. The cost of that particular style was about $12.00. I told them it would cost about $60.00 in my town. This is where Annette comes during the day.

Cindy Garris

I heard about Grace: she was a "madam" for some of these girls. Former clients were angry with her and she had to move out of her house and stay at the church for a while. Noah has security at the church and school, and they reported men were starting to harass her there as well. She has now relocated to another village but is doing well there.

When we met at the church, I told them how proud we all were of their accomplishments. They still have their Tuesday and Thursday worship time together, thanks to Ruth and Diana. We talked a long time about lots of things: The prayer requests for women in the other countries—the Congo women under the CEPAC hierarchy; the Kigondo women who have no Bibles, and the LOH women in Texas as well. We talked about the possibility that Dale and I have finished the mission in Africa and that we might not return. It was pretty intense, and we all prayed at the end. It was hard to say goodbye.

Day 38:
Noah Explains about Wedding Customs

All the women I talked to were surprised that American men don't have to pay a dowry. Because the bride's family is losing a worker, the men have to pay for her! I was surprised that their dowry requirements are so high ... five cows at least. If you are a pastor or a government official, then the dowry is higher. If a cow costs $400.00, where do they get the money? And what do they do with all the cows? This was the group at the Butare church--they thought my surprise was hysterical.

Cindy Garris

Noah said the groom and his parents have to start saving a long time. He can ask the bride to marry him before he talks to her parents, but he must still approach them and make a proposal. The Pastor makes an announcement in the church to see if anyone opposes the contract. Then you open the wedding invitation to practically the whole village!

People are supposed to help bring food if they come. They use one or two cows to kill and eat for the banquet, and they might sell another cow to help pay for everything else. They do have a wedding cake along with the prepared meal. It only takes two months from the official announcement to the actual ceremony. The bride rents a bridal gown (which the groom pays for); they rent tents and streamers, and a photographer. I have seen booths in the marketplace that advertise this as a package deal. Cops are out directing the whole affair. If you don't make a grand display, then it is

Talking With the Women

a shame to the groom that he cannot provide for his wife.

I am not sure how women in the cities go through their betrothals. But after watching the wedding parties at the Sheraton Hotel, I am certain that five cows are not the dowry requirement! Policemen stop traffic to direct the limousines and all the cars in the procession. The men wear tuxedos, the women all have on long, beautiful dresses with fancy hairdos, and there are little girls carrying flowers. A photographer is posing everyone and photographing them in strategic areas. I counted seven different wedding parties having their reception on the hotel grounds. If you have money, the Sheraton Hotel is obviously <u>the</u> place!

Cindy Garris

Day 38, 39, and 40: Kampala and then fly home.

This trip is completed. Four countries, ten churches, 35 services, and nine women's meetings! It is a 4-hour drive to Kampala from Mbarara, so we booked a room at the Sheraton and got there on Friday afternoon. Our flight home was scheduled for 11:30 PM Saturday night. Noah drove halfway there, and another driver took us through the city. Diana and a friend left Thursday night on the bus so she could meet us there and spend one last afternoon together. We passed huge fields of papyrus, sweet potatoes, and carrots. We followed a cattle truck crammed with the long-horned Ugandan cattle going to the slaughterhouse. Six or seven guys are riding on top of the cage, just laughing and talking. I watched all the little village markets for more crazy signs and logos.

We crossed the equator line and had Noah take our picture. That was pretty cool. We ate a quick bite at the café, and I watched a TV cooking show. The woman was outside cooking in her black cooking pot over an open fire! I couldn't understand what she was saying, but she was demonstrating the way she dried the cassava roots and how she made and bagged the flour. Too funny! The café had t-shirts for sale that said "Keep

Talking With the Women

Calm. You are at the Ugandan Equator!"

When we came into the city, a skinny black Santa was selling red, green & white striped umbrellas in the middle of the street. They were the little kind with short handles; he was twirling them around, walking in between the cars, saying, "Ho, Ho, Ho! Merry Christmas!"

As we walked into the Sheraton Hotel lobby, I said," Oh my gosh! It's Christmas." A tall Christmas tree was fully decorated with lights and ornaments and wrapped packages underneath. Garlands and wreaths decorated the desk, and English Christmas music was playing in the background. I felt like I was in the United States! The receptionist looked at me funny, and I said: "I have been in a banana plantation for the past two weeks. I forgot it was December!"

Cindy Garris

WALKING With the Women

Cindy Garris

Introduction

There are two kinds of walks written about in this booklet. The spiritual one with the Lord, the people in Uganda and Liberia, and the people back home. There is also the physical one: learning the customs of people in different countries, the walk up the hill to a small mountain church, surviving the rain and heat, and sharing our everyday life with each other.

Join me in a four-week journey with the Ladies of Hope and the women of Liberia! At the end of this walk, let's continue to walk together in spite of the distance and time.

Walking With the Women

THE NUMBERS!	5
THE CONFERENCES	7
Nyakashedey, Uganda	7
Ruhinda, Uganda	9
Bushenyi, Uganda	10
The Ladies of Hope –	**11**
Two Day Conference in Mbarara,	11
Kayanya Village:	144
Luwero District:	155
Kimazzi Village:	188
Christian Family Full Gospel	199
LIBERIA	**20**
Government officials,	20
Paynesville:	20
Buchanan City:	21
Buchanan City:	22
Buchanan City:	22
Paynesville:	23
Monrovia:	24
Paynesville: !	25

Cindy Garris

THE MESSAGES	**26**
AMERICAN WOMEN	**28**
AFRICAN WOMEN	**29**
THE MEN	333

Talking With the Women

THE NUMBERS!

DAYS: 30

FLIGHTS—11; HOURS—52 plus layovers

HOTELS—8

COUNTRIES—2 FOR MINISTRY + 6 TRAVELED

DISTRICTS, CITIES AND VILLAGES—12

CHURCHES REPRESENTED—30

SERVICES TOTAL— 32: WOMEN-- 14; SUNDAY, REVIVAL, AND ORDINATION—18

BIBLES DISTRIBUTED—236; $1,848.00

GOVERNMENT OFFICIALS--6

BATTLES OVERCOME — OVER 40. SOME MAJOR: lost luggage, malaria, money issues at home and here, lost/stolen phone, passion fruit land. OTHERS: normal confusion, change of plans, sickness, vehicle problems, electricity, hot water, Internet, phones, and cultural differences.

HIGHLIGHTS—MANY!! Great LOH conferences—3 sessions plus launch of new LOH groups; men's mini-meeting, Noah and Dale visiting all school and orphanage related locations. Someone wearing a Maypearl t-shirt in Luwero. A Ruhinda village that has never seen a white person.

Cindy Garris

Gift of 2 live chickens and banana stems. Victory over witchdoctors in Kayanya –Village of Love. Bible distribution and selfless sharing. Grace's Bible. Muslim woman got saved at Kasana Church. Purchased LOH items. Amazing revival services at Buchanan City, Liberia. Two healing lines with everyone getting healed in two different churches in Liberia. Smooth Jazz band at Golden Key Hotel. Daughters of Jerusalem—Oyeama's group in Hope Temple Church (Theo). A swim in the Atlantic Ocean.

Talking With the Women

THE CONFERENCES

Nyakashedey, Uganda - *Feb. 22, 2017*

About 40 women present due to a funeral that afternoon. They basically thought American women have no problems. That prompted me to tell about personal situations about women I know. We distributed 24 Bibles in their language. Because there was not enough for everyone, the leader and Diana somehow worked it out. There were no hard feelings, just laughter and joy that Bibles were available. One Bible left—two older women had their hands raised. Both pointed to the other one to get the Bible! The leader picked one woman and the other woman clapped her hands and praised the

Cindy Garris

Lord. Two women gave me a "blessing" of a 1000 UG shilling note. Exchange rate is 3500 to $1.00 USD. So that equals about 25 cents. *(Note: more Bibles were purchased the next week to give to more women at this church.)

Handing out Bibles

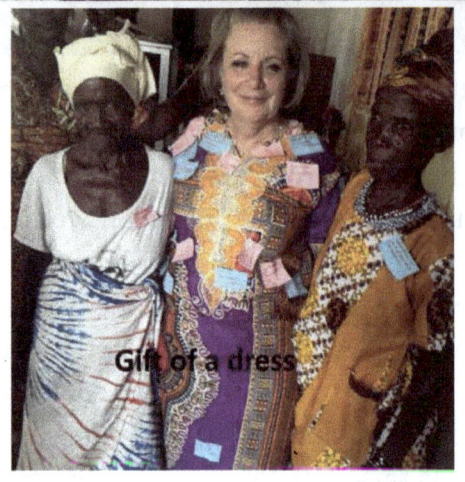

Gift of a dress

Talking With the Women

Ruhinda, Uganda - Feb. 23, 2017

The Church on the Hill! We parked the car at a building, and then Noah and Diana helped me get up a hill (mini-mountain?).

These women had never seen a white person before. It is in the middle of a coffee/sugar/banana plantation. Individual families own small plots. They harvest food for themselves and sell what they can at a market down the hill.

Chicken and Bananas

These ladies also got a case of Bibles. They served me lunch: rice, chicken broth, goat broth, goat and chicken meat, a banana dish, and fresh fruit. I declined the African tea (warm milk, tea, and sugar). I reminded Noah he didn't like Texas sweet tea. So all was well! They blessed me with a live chicken and a stem of green bananas.

Cindy Garris

Bushenyi, Uganda – Feb. 23, 2017

This is where Noah's dad's church is. We stopped for 30 minutes to visit with the women who were at the funeral and couldn't make the meeting the day before. Noah's dad asked me if I liked my walk up the hill! Then when he found out we were given a live chicken and bananas, he decided to do the same. I have met him before, but didn't realize he had such a sense of humor!

On the way back to Mbarara, I "donated" the chickens and bananas to the orphanage! Noah said he would ask if they wanted to start a chicken project or have chicken for supper! *(Two of the boys have adopted the chickens and are now learning raising poultry as a project!)

"THE WALL"—this inspiration has turned out to be a good visual explanation for women bonding and supporting each other. This also helps them in understanding how to read Bible together, have small groups, support others in prayer, teaching each other, and overcoming everyday life.

Talking With the Women

The Ladies of Hope –

Two Day Conference in Mbarara, Uganda Feb. 24 & 25

The Prayer Time and Launching of the five new LOH groups:

By this time Noah and Dale were back from the school, properties, and orphanage. So Dale and I prayed over each group and the leadership. Prayer for all the single mothers was next. The Bible distribution was a joyful time —72 Bibles! Four women who couldn't read were given Bibles with instructions to share with someone who would help them read and learn. Then Diana informed me

Cindy Garris

I had to come up with a scripture for launching the new groups. *(I had to be instantly in season!). So we went to the church office for about 15 minutes. The scripture I chose was Rev. 21: 1-7. Diana said it was perfect.

Ladies of Hope Launch

I was given a blessing: women came and gave me money or a gift. The total was 40,000 UGX Shillings (about $12.00 USD), a purse, and a necklace. These were sacrificial gifts—they had no money and they wanted to give me something. The woman took her house key out of her purse. The other woman took off her necklace and put it on me. What can you say to this?

Our second day started at 10 am and ended at 4 pm. I went to change clothes at the hotel, and then met the women at a netball field 2 blocks away from the church. They were playing against another

Talking With the Women

church group of women in their church dresses! What a great ending to an emotional, spiritual day. The score was 9-7, with the Ladies of Hope winning!

Netball with the Ladies

Cindy Garris

Kayanya Village: the Village of Love
deliverance from the witchdoctors. Sunday Service. Feb. 26, 2017

This was a Sunday Service that Dale preached. We saw the children who were earmarked for sacrifice. We saw the music pastor leading the children and congregation in worship. We heard testimonies from the different members of how deliverance came to them. The homes of the four witchdoctors who are currently in jail have been locked up. One home was destroyed. One woman witchdoctor remains in the village, but she would not respond to Dale, Noah, or the "mayor".

They would not let Dale on her property for fear of a charge and arrest of illegal trespassing. So, they stood in the middle of the street and prayed a curse over her and her house.

A gift was presented to us called a "Hima" milk jug. It is reserved for special guests who have traveled far and brought a blessing to the family. We did research when we got home, and this was a high honor. We saw the new buildings: orphanage dormitory, school, and church. We have a picture of the well and pump that have been installed for this village.

Talking With the Women

Luwero District: Kasana Church Two Ladies of Hope Conferences and two Revival Services Feb.28th and Mar. 1

Prayer at Kasana

This is a 6 hour drive from Mbarara. How do they know Noah being so far away? Family members leave a village, go to a city like Mbarara in hopes of employment, and meet Noah, Diana, and their church. They send word back to their Pastor –in this case Dao and wife Grace—who travel this long distance for inspiration and instruction.

Grace has started her own Ladies of Hope group and I purchased items to sell back home. Lydia and Anna were my translators. This church advertised the meeting as a "woman's conference", so a Muslim woman attended, who got saved that night in the revival service! I found out later that while I was praying with the women, some young woman in the back of the church starting howling and screaming. It took 5 people to restrain her until the exhibition of the demon subsided. I missed all that, but saw her lying on a straw mat asleep as I was leaving.

Kasana Church

We talked about the New Testament women again. Talked about the trials American women go through. I encouraged them to look past their "many problems" and reach out to those less fortunate than themselves.

Diana's LOH group donated four of their sewing machines to this church!

Sewing Room

Talking With the Women

Five different churches joined at this church for these two days. I stopped at Pastor Anna's church for one hour when we were driving back to Kampala and the airport. I will have more on her and her church later. Two cases of Bibles were handed out here at Kasana.

Another woman named Grace appealed to Noah for one of the new Bibles. We brought her Bible back with us to show everyone. I purchased necklaces from this newly organized LOH group.

Cindy Garris

Kimazzi Village: 9 miles from our hotel in Luwero (Nimrod Hotel) Mar. 2

Road to Kimazzi

This was a strange church. We had a ladies' meeting in the morning and one revival service in the evening. The women here travel different distances for Sunday church. Very few have their own Bibles. They have no link or communication with each other. On the contrary—they bicker, gossip, and have problems amongst themselves as well as their marriages. This is what they told me. Young women are mean to each other because they are competing for the same man. I planted the seeds. One woman in particular was excited and promised to reach out to these women.

Kimazzi church

Talking With the Women

Christian Family Full Gospel in Luwero, Pastor Anna's church Mar. 3

This was a one-hour meeting. Anna was so thankful that we stopped here on our way to Kampala and the airport. Since she was my translator at Kasana church, she had certain scriptures already written down.

She transmitted a lot to this group of 25. They asked lots of questions. The most important one was how do we support each other in the Lord? Can we do meetings like what you are doing? OF COURSE! We did "The Wall" again—only this time 8 of us were in a circle holding each other up, singing, and laughing!

Cindy Garris

LIBERIA

Ladies' Meetings, Government officials, and Revival services, March 5th

Paynesville: World Resurrection Ministries International

We are very tired. It was a difficult flight from Uganda to Liberia. It took 2 days to get from East Africa to West Africa. I was not expecting to address a Sunday morning service with full attendance of men, women, and children. I readjusted my attitude and told them as I got up to speak this was not my strong point, and please give me some grace! They did! Sandra, Momo's wife, was a big help.

Gift from Sandra

Talking With the Women

Buchanan City: New Destiny Chapel
International - Mar. 7 to Mar. 11

This whole week was amazing! We first met the City Governor and the Minister of Religious Affairs. These men were knowledgeable and on fire. Dale had 6 services here. He was able to give them a fully developed message taking them through the prophecies, scriptures, and commitment for revival. These were pastors and congregations from different churches (I think 22) in this city. The final service was the wrap-up and a healing line. Everyone was healed. Rokiatu Warner—a born-again Christian who was delivered from Islam—had a tumor on her cheek and bad eyesight. She was completely healed! Two days after, she sent another message to Dale confirming she was well.

Buchanan City: Ladies Conference at New Destiny Mar. 10

I loved this meeting. They asked honest questions and I gave honest answers. The clothes issue came up (Deut. 22:5). What should I do about an unbelieving husband? What about women pastors? What about submission to your husband? What about jewelry and fancy clothes? We all had a lively discussion with my answers and their own contributions. Tradition and cultures were discussed. They ate lunch while we all sat and talked. This lasted over three hours before I finally had to leave.

Buchanan City: Ordination Ceremony at New Destiny Mar. 11

This was very organized, official, and serious. The Biblical requirements were laid out to about 25 candidates, vows were made, and each were prayed over singly and anointed with oil. During photo time, Dale and I were given African clothes and sandals!

Talking With the Women

Paynesville: Hope Temple Church
International - March 12 – 14

It was Sunday services with Dale and then Monday for a day off. Tuesday and Wednesday, we had a 10 am Women's conference and a 6 pm Revival service. I feel like this church has some internal problems that we were unaware of. I loved the pastor's wife Oyeame. At first she seemed hard and without joy. But during the two days I spent with her, I feel she has an overwhelming load and burden for this church and the women's group that she has formed. I got the complete picture of "the bad husband" that many African women complain about. This group has not experienced a "keynote speaker" like me. I didn't "preach" to them. We interacted, we talked, and we prayed about solutions.

Cindy Garris

Monrovia: Government meetings Mar. 16th and 17th

We had about 15 minutes each with the following officials: Speaker of Legislature, Minister of Religious Affairs, Chief Protocol Officer for the President, and the Chief Officers for the Vice President. When we left Texas, we honestly didn't know if we would see any of these people. So I am excited we were able to speak with who we did.

We had special Bibles engraved, a Four Steps to Revival book, and the booklet of Dale's trip to Liberia during the Ebola epidemic.

While in Monrovia, we purchased 20 Bibles for distribution with Oyeame's group: Daughters of Jerusalem.

At the end of the day, we had our final service at Momo's church. I was presented with another African shirt and a pair of sandals!

Talking With the Women

Paynesville: Final Day in Liberia. A day at the Beach and a final meeting with the two hosting pastors!

This was a fun ending to a busy and battle-weary week. I never planned to go swimming, but the Atlantic Ocean pulled me in any way! I don't think our two pastors, our driver and his wife were expecting both me and Dale to actually get wet. I don't know if taking time off for fun with your spouse is a normal thing African couples do. But Dale and I had fun!

Cindy Garris

THE MESSAGES—

Bible Women, American Women, African Women

BIBLE WOMEN—they were examples of:

1. Enduring persecution, false accusations, ridicule, famine, death, poverty, bad husbands, war, and more—all the while trusting and believing God. And many times not seeing the reason or reward or long term plans of God—just being used as His instrument and a testimony of faith for later generations.

2. Men and women used during their lifetime in different leadership roles

3. Their service and jobs for God changed as they matured.

4. Submission: to God, a man to a woman, younger woman to older woman, woman to a man.

5. Took bold stands or defied Jewish law

6. Deliverance from demon possession or disease.

7. Disciples of Jesus—in worship, teaching, service to others

8. Raised and influenced their sons and children to be used by God

9. Evangelists

Deborah and Barak, Naomi and Ruth, Hannah,

Talking With the Women

Abigail, Joseph, David, Elizabeth and Mary, Widow with 2 mites, Woman with issue of blood, Samaritan woman, Mary Magdalene, Martha and Mary, Lois and Eunice, and Priscilla and Aquila.

I gathered all scripture references in the New Testament about women. Who were they? What was their testimony in the New Testament? Who do you relate to? During trials and hard times, can you get strength from the Lord even if you don't see the end results? You might never see the reason why. Can we overcome and be content with peace? We are saved; we are part of His bigger plan. Is it enough to persevere and know we will understand it all in heaven?

We can do different jobs at the same time. Our service to the Lord can change as we mature and circumstances change. No job for the Lord is too small. Each part of our physical body is important to make our whole body operate efficiently. If a part of our physical body is sick, we can still manage but not as well. It is the same way with the body of Christ.

Cindy Garris

AMERICAN WOMEN

I talked about women that I personally know--their particular trial, their prayer, their deliverance, and their example of faith and trust in God.

This included abusive husbands, adultery, divorce and custody issues, sickness and death, disobedient children, financial problems, our own choices that caused problems (before salvation and after salvation), and issues outside our control that cause problems.

Deliverance by: prayer and fasting, support and help from fellow church members, women sheltering women, guidance by pastors and elders

Lessons learned: more depth in God, desperate prayer, instruction and guidance from others, boldness and mercy in our faith, ability to share from our pain with others who are going through similar tests of faith.

Talking With the Women

AFRICAN WOMEN

Diana and Ruth: Noah's wife and sister. Evangelists, leaders in their church, mothers, workers, supporters of the Ladies of Hope.

Jane: a widow. The 1st woman I talked to with Diana. The Secretary and Treasurer for LOH in Mbarara.

Young wife: husband broke her arm. She came from one of the 5 districts to the conference for encouragement.

Leader from one of the districts: she came with her husband. She is 40 years old. She brought the young wife with the broken arm. She considers herself under Diana –"her spiritual mother and leader of the Ladies of Hope" and myself—"her spiritual grandmother."

Grace: from the Kasana Church in Luwero. She appealed to Noah for a new Bible.

Cindy Garris

Lydia: one of my translators at Kasana Church. Gave me a personal thank you for coming to their church and giving them instruction to be stronger women in God.

Anna: pastor and translator for me. She is 40 years old, has four sons, and has been widowed for one year. Her church building is a small wooden structure. She has already had one meeting with women in her area—not just from her church—and is planning another one in April. They are determined and excited to create a group that will sustain each other in their walk with Jesus and working through their poverty.

Grace—another one! This is the lady in the orange dress at the Kimazzi Village church. She understood the need for these women to overcome their differences, support each other, and read with each other. She promised to give Bibles to those who would read and share.

Talking With the Women

Sandra Seeley: Pastor Momo's wife. She gave me peace and encouragement when I had to speak at the Sunday morning service. She has a ministry called Care for Every Woman and Child. Their goal is clean water, support, protect, and give Biblical instruction to women, and provide necessary daily life needs.

A young woman: spiritual "daughter"of Sandra. Her husband left here and took the 2 children. She has a disease in her legs that has discolored and raised welts on her. When Dale prayed over her, she collapsed on the floor and went into a fit. Sandra, women, and Dale prayed over her. When Dale touched her hand, she calmed down immediately.

Oyeame Wesseh: Pastor Theo's wife. At first I was unsure about her, but getting to know her after two days made me realize she has a strong burden and heart for the women. Her organization is 4 years old: Daughters of Jerusalem. There are 21 churches aligned with her and giving support to women in their district. They have added literacy to their list of projects: self-employment, Bible accountability, and more.

Sandy O'phelia: the Vice President of the Daughters of Jerusalem. She gave her testimony during the first conference. A prostitute who was redeemed and reaching out to women in the same situation she was in. She is now married; both her husband and her serving in many ways in a ministry.

Rokiatu Warner: A pastor, apostle, and leader in her church. She was in the healing line and was healed from a tumor in her cheek and bad eyesight.

Rokiatu, Mom, and Me

Talking With the Women

THE MEN

— these were the women's answers as to why there are so many bad husbands

1. You are married for a long time. Then he sees a younger woman and leaves. He feels no responsibility for his children or wife
2. He is a church goer but gets in with the wrong crowd (through work, travel, etc.). He stops going to church but stays with his family while he commits adultery.
3. A wife won't submit, won't listen, won't work, and won't be responsible, so husband turns bad.
4. The wife wants lots of babies and feels that will keep her husband. He feels pressure of no money and wants to leave.
5. You are married for a long time. He sees younger girls still in shape wearing seductive clothes. Wants you to dress and act the same way. But you won't submit in that way. So, he leaves.
6. He can't take the pressure of a family, so he leaves—expects the wife to take all responsibility of money for kids.
7. You are married; wife gets saved, but he doesn't. He either leaves or abuses the wife.
8. Women substitute and idolize the husband instead of Jesus. She gets disappointed and starts being a bitter woman.

9. Even though there is a law (in Liberia) for the father to take responsibility for his family, it is not enforced. The wife can file a complaint, but if the husband bribes the police, they let him go.

RevivalFire Ministries

PO Box 822
Waxahachie, TX 75168
Cgarris54@gmail.com
http://Revivalfire.org

www.ingramcontent.com/pod-product-compliance
Lightning Source LLC
Chambersburg PA
CBHW070450050426
42451CB00015B/3428